DISNEY MOVIE FAVORITES

CONTENTS

© THE WALT DISNEY COMPANY

ISBN 978-0-7935-2092-3

HAL•LEONARD®
CORPORATION
7777 W BLUEMOUND RD. P.O. BOX 13819 MILWAUKEE, WI 53213

DAUGHTERS OF TRITON
(From Walt Disney's "THE LITTLE MERMAID")

Lyrics by HOWARD ASHMAN
Music by ALAN MENKEN

FATHOMS BELOW
(From Walt Disney's "THE LITTLE MERMAID")

Lyrics by HOWARD ASHMAN
Music by ALAN MENKEN

KISS THE GIRL
(From Walt Disney's "THE LITTLE MERMAID")

Lyrics by HOWARD ASHMAN
Music by ALAN MENKEN

Moderately

PART OF YOUR WORLD
(From Walt Disney's "THE LITTLE MERMAID")

Lyrics by HOWARD ASHMAN
Music by ALAN MENKEN

Moderately bright

7

UNDER THE SEA
(From Walt Disney's "THE LITTLE MERMAID")

Lyrics by HOWARD ASHMAN
Music by ALAN MENKEN

Brightly

BELLE
(From Walt Disney's "BEAUTY AND THE BEAST")

Lyrics by HOWARD ASHMAN
Music by ALAN MENKEN

GASTON
(From Walt Disney's "BEAUTY AND THE BEAST")

Lyrics by HOWARD ASHMAN
Music by ALAN MENKEN

BE OUR GUEST
(From Walt Disney's "BEAUTY AND THE BEAST")

Lyrics by HOWARD ASHMAN
Music by ALAN MENKEN

SOMETHING THERE
(From Walt Disney's "BEAUTY AND THE BEAST")

Lyrics by HOWARD ASHMAN
Music by ALAN MENKEN

THE MOB SONG
(From Walt Disney's "BEAUTY AND THE BEAST")

Lyrics by HOWARD ASHMAN
Music by ALAN MENKEN

BEAUTY AND THE BEAST
(From Walt Disney's "BEAUTY AND THE BEAST")

Lyrics by HOWARD ASHMAN
Music by ALAN MENKEN

Lyrically

ARABIAN NIGHTS
(From Walt Disney's "ALADDIN")

Words by HOWARD ASHMAN
Music by ALAN MENKEN

FRIEND LIKE ME
(From Walt Disney's "ALADDIN")

Words by HOWARD ASHMAN
Music by ALAN MENKEN

ONE JUMP AHEAD
(From Walt Disney's "ALADDIN")

Music by ALAN MENKEN
Words by TIM RICE

A WHOLE NEW WORLD
(From Walt Disney's "ALADDIN")

Music by ALAN MENKEN
Words by TIM RICE

PRINCE ALI
(From Walt Disney's "ALADDIN")

Lyrics by HOWARD ASHMAN
Music by ALAN MENKEN